DOT MARKERS
ACTIVITY BOOK

COLORED BY

_____

_____

This dot marker activity coloring book includes over 40 illustrations, black and white designs to color by kids, toddlers of 2+ years, great for children who love to celebrate easter with beautiful rabbits and eggs.
40 coloring pages with amazing drawings will let you enter in a world of joy and entertainment.
After each coloring page you have a blank page which is added to try your own drawings if you wanted to practice your skills. These blank pages also help you avoid damaging other pages while using pens or markers that bleed through paper.
I greatly appreciate you for purchasing this book, and I hope you really enjoy it, if so, please don't hesitate to give a feedback and a review, that will mean a lot to me as an artist and it really motivates and helps creating more good content.

L'BRIGHTSIDE EASTER DRAWINGS
Copyright © 2021
All rights reserved

COLOR TEST DOTS

CPSIA information can be obtained
at www.ICGtesting.com
Printed in the USA
LVHW060218290323
742928LV00011B/615